HOW TO CHOOSE YOUR CAREER PATH

A SELF-GUIDED BOOK, JUST FOR YOU

ANURADHA MANDAL

In loving memory of my *Uncle Kundu Kaku.*

With a full heart, I humbly dedicate this work to you, my wonderful readers, my parents, and my teachers

Contents

Preface

This book is dedicated to each one-off you. One who is on the verge of completing their school education, the undergraduates, the young graduates, the entry-level and the mid-level professionals One who wants to get clarity on how to choose their career path and become successful.

Purpose for the reader: To help and encourage individuals to learn the exact meaning of a Career and its importance while also helping them with the best-suited roadmap for their career.

What if I tell you that one word, *"Can Make You or Break You"*?

And this has nothing to do with rocket science, but this has to do with every individual's life.

You must be curious about it.

Right?

And what if I tell you that this will make your life more *"Meaningful at the same time Happier"?*

Would that make you read this book fully?

If you do not believe it, it is possible that you are the person who would benefit most from this book.

And I recommend that you complete the book before considering not taking your career seriously. If you choose the right career from the very beginning of your career journey, you will resonate with this.

But unfortunately, this is not true with most individuals.

Most of you do not take it seriously and later repent over the decision.

This book has information on how important one's career is and how one should make the most out of it.

"Trust me, this is true, and this has been proven."

It's not just information but a fact, because I know 1000s of students and professionals who make wrong decisions in choosing their career and later regret their decision.

And it's not like it's too late for you.

It is just when you realize and when you are ready to take the charge of your life.

I see so many students and young professionals grind their life in careers not suited for them. They feel stuck in their so-called career and are hesitant to give a new start with a fresh choice. The choice which will make them more successful, accomplished, happy, and rich.

If you have picked up this book, it means that you have heard about the importance of a career already and have some belief that you can carve your career in your own way.

Now it is time to make it a reality.

This is easy.

Believe me, this is very easy because this has nothing to do with huge investments or tough competition.

This has to do only with your passion, interest, choice, and clarity.

Though it is easy, you cannot expect to declare yourself as a victorious person one fine day and expect a successful career to fall in your lap.

A career means a part of your life. A career is a combination of education, roles, experiences, and the pathway you take to achieve your objective.

It takes time, energy, and coherence in learning about all these.

But it is an investment that is worth it.

And this would produce exponential results in the future.

That's what we are going to discuss in this book.

I am going to get your feet wet in the career path journey so that you get complete intelligibility with it.

Once you start this you will have lucidity, you will be motivated to learn more about your career journey, and you will go more deeply into it yourself.

This book is designed to give you that first small win.

Imagine how it would feel when you get into your dream college, your dream university, or your dream job in your dream company.

Until that happens, you are not going to believe in this approach. So, forget about everything that you have heard about the career, and let's focus on getting your best-suited career path.

That should be your goal and that's my goal as well to help you reach there through the information in this book.

So, let's jump into it.

CHAPTER ONE

SUCCESS MINDSET

Your Mindset is Everything.

A beautiful day begins with a beautiful mindset.

Have you ever thought?

Why one person is happy and another sad?

Why one person is confident, and another not very confident?

Have you ever wondered?

What sets those who get huge success, and others failing?

Why one person can network well in a group, and another can't talk to a stranger?

What sets those who achieve great things apart from those who fail to realize their aspirations?

Have you pondered on it?

Why do one person with a great education, and skills, struggle in their career, and another person with lesser knowledge or skills grow in his/her career?

You might be thinking that the answer to all the above questions is intelligence, aptitude, creativity, or risk appetite.

All those are sensible suggestions.

But that's not what science has found.

According to **Stanford psychologist***Carol Dweck* and others, the predictor of Success in Life is none of the above sensible suggestions.

But it is the mindset.

It's your Mindset.

> *"The mind is everything. What you think, you become.---Buddha."*

According to the Oxford Dictionary- Mindset is a set of attitudes or fixed ideas that someone has and that is often difficult to change.

People with a **"Growth Mindset"** are the ones who achieve great things generally by believing that they can improve and grow as people.

While the people with a **"Fixed Mindset"** are the ones who put a stop to their attempts to realize their dreams and tend to believe their abilities, talents, and potential to be static/stable.

FIXED MINDSET	GROWTH MINDSET
I am either good at something or I am not	I can work and improve my skills with practice and hard work
I am criticized when people give me feedback	I respect when people give me feedback. It helps me improve, learn, and grow.
Successful people are lucky and never experienced failure	Successful people have failed many a time, but they did not quit until they achieved success

In this book, you will get insights into your Success Mindset in the context of your successful career journey.

Having a success mindset means having a mind that's ready to work towards achieving your goals despite the odds you might encounter.

Your mind speaks different languages, one is agile, and another is slow in its corners.

It speaks different languages when it comes to what you want to do in your career.

So, what you want to do, you must think deeply and think clearly because it is very important thinking?

Thinking clearly doesn't mean what will I get from this or what will I get from that.

It's your life and your life is precious.

Ask this question to yourself.

Is your life precious to you?

If yes.

Then before investing this life into something, you must think today, that if I invest my life into this then after 20 years will it mean a lot to me?

After 40 years will it still mean a lot to me?

And at the end of my life when I turn back and narrate.

Will I be proud of this 'or will I be ashamed of what I was doing?

It doesn't matter what other people are saying.

But you shouldn't do anything that you will be ashamed of.

Isn't it?

It doesn't matter people say so many things.

Everybody has an opinion, and it is their business.

But you should not do anything that you feel ashamed of.

This much pride and freedom you must keep in your life.

So, this is all you must look at.

Remember one thing.

Something will get you money.

Something will get you comfort.

That's not the point.

What you choose to do.

Will it give life to you?

When I say, life.

Are you just trying to make a living or are you trying to make a life out of this?

See ....

Making a living is not an issue. Even a bird, an insect, a worm, a bee, or an animal is making their life and making their living.

Isn't it?

Making a living with a big brain is not an issue, earning your food is again not a problem.

But the only problem is

You want to live like somebody else.

That is an endless problem.

You want to live like others – this is a real problem.

And this creates pressure.

It's very usual to hear that your father has a dream, he wants you to become an engineer. Your mother dreamt that you should become a doctor.

Please understand that this is their dream, and they are not going to live your life.

Look I am not saying that we shouldn't fulfill your parent's dreams,

They are the most amazing people; they gave birth to us they grew us up they did so much for us, and we have a duty out of our genuine love and gratitude to serve them.

But when you come under pressure. You get puzzled and get distracted from your path. When you get distracted.

One thing that you all should do, is to withdraw yourself.

Yes, you heard it right.

Withdraw yourself from the pressure of peers, professors, parents, and everybody before making a big decision in your life.

Take and spend some time of your life, maybe one week and look at it.

Look at it, what is it that, you want to invest this precious life into.

What is it that will be worthwhile today and worthwhile after 50 years for you to invest?

Invest your life into that, whatever it is, however small or big it is, it doesn't matter

What it is that you really want to do and not under the pressure from other people matters.

Do that.

It doesn't matter what other people think about it.

A whole lot of people today are deciding what to do depending on what they will get out of it.

Will I get this kind of lifestyle?

Will I get that kind of salary?

Will I make this kind of money?

This is the wrong approach.

Because this approach will have you everything, but you will have nothing at the end of life.

There will be no fulfillment in life. You will live a very poor life and there will be no growth.

The greatest killer of our growth is what society thinks we should be doing.

There are social standards of what you should be doing, socially it's cool to have a job or a business.

Again, as a social standard, you should have a home at a certain location, have a certain car, wear certain kinds of clothes, and have a certain kind of hairstyle.

And we give so much importance to it because we want to be socially accepted.

In this whole gamut of social acceptance, we forget to make a simple calculation.

And this calculation is very important and is an eye-opener.

Assume you spend 8 hrs. at work daily.

It's a very conservative number though, we spend way more than this.

If you work for 8 hrs. daily and you are working 5 days a week, that is 40 hrs. per week at work.

And assuming you took 2 weeks off holiday every year that is 50 weeks working.

That comes down to 2000 hrs. of yours at work.

And assuming you work for 45 yrs., then the further calculation comes down to 90000 hrs. of your life at work.

90000 hrs. seem to be a daunting number.

That's the average of 10 yrs. of your life.

You need to be very sure whether you want to get into this 90000 hrs. of dissatisfaction or 90000 hrs. of cribbing and complaining

A very common statement you must have heard from your surroundings.

Saying I don't like it.

This is not what I wanted to do

Or

This is what my parents wanted.

Just because you are getting paid or in some cases getting paid more, you cannot be miserable for those 90000 hrs.

Furthermore, you can never achieve excellence.

Excellence only comes when you do something which truly resonates with your soul. You can be good at it. But it may not be fulfilling for you.

So, you need to be very wise while choosing your path, whether it's a career path or your life path. It is the most precious path of your precious life.

"If you change the way you look at things, the things you look at change-Wayne Dyer."

Change Your State Of Mind

Anthony Robbins says that lasting change occurs when you are in an altered state. That is why he created 22 ways to instantly change your state. You can change your state by following simple actions.

1. **Fun**- Fun is enjoyment, and fun is amusement. Having fun helps you to forget your worries. Do something just forfun.
2. **Freedom**- Freedom is the state of being free. Take a ferry ride, cruise on a yacht, dive in the water, or go for a long drive in your favorite car or motorbike.
3. **Relax & Read**- Become less tense or anxious. Books and articles change your state into a state of joy, happiness, and gratitude by reading books or articles.
4. **Movement**- A movement is an act of moving or slight movement in the body. Movement of any kind changes your state.
5. **Words**- Words are powerful. Word either gives us energy or depletes our energy. Notice the words you use when speaking.
6. **Meditate**- Meditation is a vital way to purify and calm the mind. Meditation helps in rejuvenating the body
7. **Laugh**- Laugh is the best medicine. Always laugh when you can. Children laugh an average of 300 times per day when compared with an adult
8. **Best Friend**- Spending time with your buddies brings joy and positivity. Try and make out most of it.
9. **Smile**- Smile is free therapy. A smile improves your mood. Recent studies say that smiling often rewires your brain to create a more positive design.
10. **Journaling**- Journaling is writing in a journal or diary. Impacts on your physical health and helps in the removal of mental blocks, start journaling.
11. **Heart**- A good Heart keeps you beautiful. Practice the art of gratitude daily to remain present, appreciative, and positive.

12.   **Think Big-** You have to think big to be big. Think big in life no one is stopping you from thinking big.

13.   **Review-** Review is essential for evaluation which is essential to progress. It's time for you to review.

14.   **Your Nearest and Dearest-** Talk to the nearest and dearest one. They help us reach a resolution; they often can see something we have overlooked.

15.   **Nature-** Nature is the best spiritual teacher. Nature has the power to bring empathy, love, and emotional stability.

16.   **Give-** A phenomenal way to change your mood is to think about someone else. Help an elderly person cross the road, stand up and give a seat to the needed one on the bus, and volunteer in a charity organization.

17.   **Change of Scenery-** Looking forward to, shifts your thoughts to the future and gives you something to be excited about it.

18.   **Get in The Ring-** Exercise is a great stress releaser and creates wonders. Indulge in any form of workout.

19.   **Challenge-** Challenge yourself, it is the only path that leads to growth. Set a new challenge to change your focus and excel in that different direction.

20.   **Drink-** Many studies have proven that increasing your water intake improves your mood. Aim to drink an average of 2 liters daily.

21.   **Chill-** Chill is a mental mould. Do not take things too seriously. It's time to take a chill.

22.   **Change-** Change is inevitable. Change is constant. By doing different things and changing your routine, you change your life.

The change in your state of mind will make you go through various emotional levels. You experience all levels of emotional state.

It is very important to know the state of the emotional level.

****

Emotional Guidance Scale

Abraham-Hicks has described 22 emotions and he has described them on an emotional scale.

Here are the 22 most felt emotions, and as you go through the scale you understand, that individuals with the higher up the scale, are the happier, and the lower on the scale, are the unhappier ones.

So, what you need to do, is that you find the emotion where you are now.

And you speak, think, figure out and try to move up on the scale, one emotion at a time.

1. Joy/Appreciation/Empowered/Freedom/Love
2. Passion
3. Enthusiasm/Eagerness/Happiness
4. Positive Expectation/Belief
5. Optimism
6. Hopefulness
7. Contentment
8. Boredom
9. Pessimism
10. Frustration/Irritation/Impatience
11. Overwhelmed
12. Disappointment
13. Doubt
14. Worry
15. Blame
16. Discouragement
17. Anger

18. Revenge
19. Hatred/Rage
20. Jealousy
21. Insecurity/Guilt/Unworthiness
22. Fear/Grief/Depression/Despair/Powerlessness

Let's understand and practice together. For example:

Let's say you feel **"depressed"** *(Emotion-22)*. You cannot improve your emotion, by jumping to

(Emotion-1) at once, in fact, it would be very hard to do that.

So, what you can do is you could think of thoughts that create feelings of perhaps **"guilt"***(Emotion-21)* within you. Stay in that emotional state for some time till the time you really feel it, then climb up.

Now you can create feelings of **"rage"***(Emotion-19)* within you with your thoughts.

Further on you can feel **"blame"***(Emotion-15)*, and then *"disappointment"* *(Emotion-12),* and so on.

Every emotion is an improvement, and you will always have to go upwards toward emotional number 1 which is - Joy/Appreciation/Empowered/ Freedom/Love

Try not to be at the lower part of the emotional scale, look through it and try to get to least number 7

You can make yourself feel differently with the right kind of thoughts and with the right kind of measurement.

Measure Everything

Measurement is very important.

"What gets measured, gets managed"

Just Imagine

Someone or maybe you walk into the gym, warm-up, hop on to a few machines, do a little bit of this exercise, does a little bit of that exercise, finish the workout, and leave the gym.

So, what is notable about this situation?

The person who has not measured anything has no basis for knowing if the individual is making progress or not.

Not tracking one's progress is one of the major mistakes.

We all have areas of life that we say are important to us, but we aren't measuring that.

As we know the things, we measure are the things we improve. It is through numbers and proper tracking that we get the idea of whether we are getting better or worse.

Our lives are shaped by how we choose to spend our time and energy each day.

Measuring can help us spend that time in better ways, more consistently.

Again, you can't measure everything like Love, Morality, etc.

That's true.

But even for things that can't be quantified, measuring can be helpful.

And it doesn't have to be complicated or time-consuming.

You can't measure love, but you can trackways that you are showing up with love in your life.

Send a digital love note to your parents or love done each day (text, email, voicemail, tweet)

Now that you have received some information regarding success mindset, change of state of mind, emotional state, and measurement.

You need to rethink it in context to your career path journey and make the best use of it before making a concrete career decision.

Let's dive in a bit more to understand the meaning and myth associated with a career.

CHAPTER TWO

Career-The Meaning & Myth

A career refers to a profession, occupation, or trade.

A career is defined as what you do for a living and encompasses those that require training and education. A career means working as a doctor, lawyer, teacher, carpenter, engineer, electrician, accountant, teacher, chef, or hairstylist.

"Every Day Is The Beginning Of Your Career.--- Pat McGrath"

Career has another meaning as well.

It also refers to the advancements and actions you have taken throughout the working years of your life, especially those related to your occupation. It may consist of the different jobs you have done, the titles you have earned, and the work you have carried out over a long period of time. When observed in this context, a career includes everything related to your career development, including your profession and progression.

In a simple language.

A career is what you do for a living and how you advance through a profession or company.

You can also say.

A career is an occupation or profession that one undertakes for a longer period in one's life and derives a monetary benefit from it.

Let's take an example to understand the meaning of a career in a layman's language.

Assuming you are good at astrology but do not gain any monetary benefits from it, then this will be considered your hobby and not your career.

But, if you start consulting clients and start getting some reward out of it, then Astrology becomes your Career.

Let's put this example in a different way.

Suppose you are very good at painting, but you are not displaying your talent and skill of painting and hence not gaining any pecuniary benefits from it, then this painting will be again considered as your recreation and not as your Career.

Similarly, if you start showcasing your artwork in exhibitions, art fairs, and festivals and start getting some financial reward out of it, then painting becomes your Career.

The career life of most individuals on average is around 40 years.

You are going to invest 80% of your life's time in the job or business which we call a Career.

According to career change statistics, an average person changes their career about 5-7 times in their working life.

The study also shows that 80% of working professionals are not happy and satisfied with the work they are doing. There is a tendency to change the career even after 10-15 years of experience.

As per the survey, 93% of Indian students are aware of only seven career options out of 250+ career options available.

The figures and numbers are quite daunting, but this is the reality. This reality becomes more vulnerable when it gets encapsulated with prevailing myths.

There are myths in almost everything surrounding us, and a career is not an exception.

Career Myth #1

"There is one perfect job for me."

Fact: You can find various fulfilling careers in your domain. And after you become interested in a particular career field, you can also pursue different career paths. If you are interested in working in education, then you can narrow your focus to a particular forte, such as a schoolteacher, professor, administrator, counselor, etc., and weigh the pro and cons of each job. Over time people's interests change. It's not uncommon for someone who graduated from college with a degree in physics, later in life they've developed an interest in agriculture. The most suited job today may not be the suited job tomorrow.

Career Myth #2

"My specialization or major is going to define my career."

Fact: You must have seen many of your known or you yourself may be working in a profile that is not related to what you have studied in college. Some companies such as engineering, law, etc. recruit, and look for individuals who have certain majors when it is necessary for the performance of the job duties. Companies usually place more emphasis on previous work experience and skillsets when compared to majors or specializations.

Career Myth#3

"There is only one career in my lifetime."

Fact: People go through several career changes throughout the course of their working lives. This is something very relevant and a common occurrence. In fact, people experience 5 career transitions during their lives. This can be because of economic changes or personal reasons. Since it is hard to determine whether a career will be long-term or not, you need to find a career that interests you and evaluate it after working for a while.

Career Myth#4

"Liberal Arts and Humanities majors are usually unemployable after College."

Fact: Only engineers, doctors, etc. are employable after college. Those who have completed liberal arts and humanities programs usually get into writing, and research skills. But these skills can be applied in several ways in different industries

Career Myth#5

"Most students are aware of their career goals when they enter college."

Fact: This may be true for some, but most college students change their majors and career focuses or paths many times. It is found that college students switch majors 3 to 5 times during college. This practice continues in the job as well. Professionals are also seen switching their job and career often frequently.

Career Myth#6

"Career assessment tests are the tool for choosing the right career."
Fact: Career assessments are useful in determining and finding out your career interests, but these tests will certainly not tell you which career is best for you. You answer a variety of questions during a career assessment and get a general idea of what type of career you should pursue. However, many factors are not accounted for in a career assessment. After completing an assessment, you get a good idea to critically analyze the results before pursuing a specific career path.

Career Myth#7

"Always choose an occupation based on the strongest skills."
Fact: Your personal job skillsets should not be the only factor to consider while making career decisions. Other important parameters should also be taken into consideration like interests, work environment, and earning potential. Choosing a career based only on individual talents will not equate to career satisfaction.

Career Myth#8

"I can't change my career after years in a particular field."
Fact: Rather than killing yourself in your so-called Career. It is better to take charge of your life and give it a new start. The only thing that can help you overcome this is to start.

Career Myth#9

"I should focus on a career that's job security and is in demand."
Fact: The demand for the job depends on the current and future projection and these should be treated as some sort of signal. For example, currently, there is a huge demand for Data Scientists. And therefore, lots of students are deciding to pursue their careers in this field. Well, there is a demand now, and people are pursuing careers solely based on the

current market movement. There will be demand and supply issues across the industries and saturation will come. Hence while choosing a career path have many signals in mind and future projection should play a small role in your decision.

Career Myth#10

"Becoming an entrepreneur or working on my own will give me satisfaction and happiness."

Fact: "Grass is greener from the other side" Same holds very true when you become an entrepreneur or start working on your own. You get the real feel only once you get into that shoe. So, decide wisely before taking that extraordinary step.

As you have reached this part of the book. You must be having a good understanding of the meaning of a career and what are the myths associated with a career.

Now it's time for you to take a step forward and assess yourself.

The next chapter will guide you to assess yourself and other connecting factors necessary for the best suitable options for you.

CHAPTER THREE

ASSESS YOURSELF

Assessing oneself is by far the most important activity.

And this can be done by assessing your own skill and this helps you in all possible ways to make a cemented decision.

Assessment can be done by any skill assessment test.

"The Future Depends on What You Do Today-Mahatma Gandhi"

A skill assessment can be helpful at any stage of your career, whether you start your career, progress in your career, or return to your career.

Assess what you are good at?

Assess what you like to do?

Assess and find out market needs, and opportunities associated with your skills?

Assess and find out which careers might be right for you.

This will give direction to you and will help in creating a roadmap for you. And while doing so three prominent parameters will come into the picture. These three are interest, aptitudes, and values.

Interests are basically what you like to do.

Figuring out your interest plays a vital role in this.

Aptitude is the natural qualities or talents that you have. It is a component of competence to do a kind of job at a certain level.

Skill is the ability to do something very well because of training, practice, and experience.

Work values are principles or beliefs related to your career or work. Knowing your work value will make you more confident and you enjoy a satisfying career.

Putting It Together. Let's concoct and find out the best in you. Make a list of all those things you are good at.

Come on.

You know it, right.

Each one of us is good at some or another thing.

You can be good at writing,

You can be good at singing,

You can be good at studying

You can be good at talking to your friends,

You can be good at planning,

and You can be good at many things.

Make a listicle of the things. Then ask yourself one question.

Of the list of all the things that you are good at, how much do you enjoy doing that thing?

Because it is not necessary that if you are good at something you will also enjoy doing that thing.

You may be good at planning, but you get tired while executing it, thus you may not enjoy planning.

Decipher the thing you are good at and at the same time you feel happy while doing that thing. Find out the passion in you.

Again, ask yourself a question?

Can your passion be converted into something that people need?

Can your passion be converted into something that people are looking for?

Let's take an example

You are good at digital marketing, and you get pleasure and happiness in digital marketing stuff.

Now ask yourself.

Can you convert this passion into something that the people of the world are in need of?

The answer to it is a big yes.

You know there is a huge demand for digital marketers in this arena of the digital world. People want to learn and study digital marketing to develop their skills.

People want to make a career in digital marketing.

People want to make use of digital marketing in their business,

People want to use it for personal branding.

This very simple exercise will give you direction where you will realize what you are good at and what makes you happy and at the same time something that the world needs.

When you get the intersection of these three things you will get the first hope or vision about what your career could be.

Now that you have figured out the intersection. You need to find out how these things are done in the world.

How does the expert in the world do this?

Of all the topmost digital marketers in the world, your approach is to dig out what did they do in their lives and their careers?

And how did they do it?

Always remember, that when you are talking about a career, then you should not be thinking about only the financial part of it.

It may be possible, and it is recommended that you have two parallel lives.

One in which you are doing a job, and you are doing just and taking care of your money, like paying your bills, and whatever expense you have in your life, you are fulfilling it.

But there is a second parallel life, which is taking care of the passion you are pursuing and trying to make that career.

It is quite possible that from the very first day of your digital marketing you will not start earning.

And you will have to pursue a job because that is a necessity. However, that job will not be there to fulfill your desire, rather it will be your survival. Maybe this job will not get you your dream house, dream car, and other expensive things.

However, along with this job, if you are able to convert your passion in one, two, or three years into something that the world needs, then you will start making money from it ultimately.

It can be anything and in today's world, everything is possible. You can be a basic logo designer also; you can make it a career. However, that will not happen on day one.

And if you put pressure on monetization on your passion from day one then unfortunately that will never turn into your career.

That passion will remain as a hobby and pastime engagement. You have to convert your passion into a career out of it.

If you can convert things that you are good at, which you are happy to do and if you can convert that thing for what the world needs, then it can become your career.

But to reach that career, you probably need a job. Not probably rather certainly you need a job.

Do not neglect or dismiss your that job, respect that job, however, do not make it the reason for your existence.

Definitely do not use it for your desires, just use it for your survival.

And then whatever time you can utilize, use it to shape your career. In addition to the above-mentioned crucial exercise, you can take a skill assessment test.

These skill assessments are tools to help you learn more about yourself. These assessments will help you identify your skills, interests, and values. It helps in finding the career that fits you the best. The assessment can tell you what you already know about yourself.

Before taking these assessments, you should also have a clear understanding of what an assessment can't tell you.

A career or a skill assessment test will not tell you whether a particular job will make you happy. This will not tell you whether a job will be satisfying for you or will it motivate you. Assessment tests are an evaluation of an individual's ability to perform a particular skill or set of skills.

Please understand, that a job is more than the skills needed to do the job. It involves organization, team members, boss, salary, office culture, and commute.

All these things together or in combination can influence how you feel about your work.

There are various types of skill assessment tests available, and it is highly and largely advisable to take these assessments. Some of the skill assessment tests are highlighted below:

- **Hard Skills Assessment**
- **Combination Approach**
- **Cognitive Ability Test**
- **Psychometric Test**
- **Personality Test**

This test assesses and covers all aspects of individual evaluation in a very holistic way. Some of the examples of Skill Assessment tests are:

- *Question -Answer Test*

- *Problem-solving Test*
- *Work samples and simulations or a work sample test*
- *Role-playing test or Role play exercises.*

Now that you have a fair idea of interest, aptitude, skills, and values. **What are you waiting for?**

Execute the same in your life and come up with your own set of interests and skills.

CHAPTER FOUR

SET GOAL & CREATE PLAN

What are Goals?

Goals are the things you want to achieve and accomplish in your life. Goals give you direction, motivation, and self-confidence.

Most of the time your final objective or goal seems to be very large and hard to achieve. Breaking it down into small steps and planning will help you achieve the goal.

At present, right now, you may not know what career you will end up choosing.

You may not know which options will help you get there. But you need to explore and take action to find the best fit for you.

The fit can be for now and later. And this can be done by setting your goals.

> *"If you don't know where you are going, how can you expect to get there?*
>
> *-Basil S. Walsh"*

Goals can be short-term, or long-term. Goals that happen quickly are called short-term goals.

Short term goal is a goal you want to do soon like today, this week, this month, or this year. A short-term goal is a goal you can achieve in 12 months or less time.

Examples of short-term goals

- *Take an online course.*
- *Exercise regularly.*
- *Drink more water.*
- *Read more books.*
- *Join a driving class.*
- *But a new mobile.*

Goals that take a sufficiently long time to achieve are called long-term goals. A long-term goal is what you want to do in the future. Long-term goals cannot be done in this week, this month, or even this year. It requires time and planning.

Examples of long-term goals

- *Graduating from a college.*
- *Learn a foreign language.*
- *Starting your own business.*
- *Buy your own property.*
- *Save up for retirement.*
- *Live a healthy life.*

How To Set Your Long-Term Goals

Work backward:

Have deep thinking about what you want to achieve and then plan steps going back to what you can do right now in the present scenario.

Visualize and create a picture of where you want to reach in life 10 years down the lane.

Think about your plan for the next years from now. Think again about your plan in one year and in six months from now to get to your long-term goals.

Make a note or write down what you need to do each month to accomplish your goals. Once the monthly goal is achieved, look at your goals and adjust as needed.

How you adjust your goal is very crucial and this is where prioritizing your goals comes into the picture.

Prioritizing means what is most important for you right now. All your goals are important, but it is almost impossible to work on all of them at once.

Hence, choose the most important one now and focus on that goal solely.

You can change your focus on the goals as your life changes and you will very make it out.

Be smart while setting your goals. **SMART** goals mean.

- **Specific:** means precise. Write out clear and concise goals. Example: Instead of saying "I want to be healthy". A specific goal can be "I'm going to exercise and meditate daily".
- **Measurable:** It is the ability to track your progress. Example: Instead of saying "I will lose weight". A measurable goal is "I 'm going to lose 15 pounds".
- **Achievable:** It means your goal is within your reach. Set challenging yet achievable goals. Example: Instead of saying: "I'm going for rigorous exercise". An achievable goal is "I'm going to take half an hour walks every day".
- **Relevant:** It means relevancy. The set goal that is relevant to your overall life plan. Realistic is the possibility to do work within a fixed timeframe. Example: Instead of saying: "I'm going to lose 15 pounds in 10 days". A realistic goal is "I'm going to lose two pounds in a week"
- **Time-based:** It means the goal is not open-ended. It has a target time to finish. Example: Instead of saying:" I'm going to lose 15 pounds". A time-based goal is: "I'm going to lose 15 pounds in 3 months".

****

Successful Transition To A Career

This is done by a career plan.

What is Career Plan?

A Career plan is a hands-on approach to decide your interest and skills, putting down career goals, and planting actions in place that will help you achieve them. It is a continuous process that ensures that your career is moving in the right direction.

Simple steps to design your Career Plan

1. Recognize your Career Options.

Make a list of career options based on your skills, interest, values, and strength. Narrow down the listed career options by researching companies, market opportunities, demand, salary company culture, and talking to professionals in the fields. You can further narrow it down by participating or taking experience through an internship, training, or volunteering.

2. Rank or prioritize.

It is not sufficient to list down or identify options. You have to rank them. Now you need to prioritize them based on your skills, and interests. For example.

- *What skills do you have?*
- *What interests and values you the most?*
- *What is cardinal to you?*
- *Whether it needs sound aptitude or intellectually challenging work?*
- *Will it bring a big paycheck?*

3. Drive comparison.

Make and compare your promising career options against the list of your prioritized interest, skillsets, strength, and values. Also, consider factors beyond personal bent or fondness.

4. Make a Choice.

Choosing the career path best suited for you is crucial. How many paths you choose depends upon your capabilities, situation, and comfort level. At a nascent stage of your career plan, you can pick out multiple options. You can have several paths to increase the chance of a lot of potential opportunities. Conversely tapering to one or two options will focus on a better higher study or job search.

5. Set SMART goals

- S-Specific.
- M-Measurable.
- A-Attainable.
- R-Relevant.
- T-Time-bound.

Sample Of Career Plan

Long-term career goal: **To become a Data Scientist.**

Short-term activities include the following activities.

Learn more about this specific field: Talk with three people in this career to develop a list of realistic activities within one month.

- **Develop related skills:** Take a certification program or learn a programming language within six months.
-
- **Practice skills:** Use the software at work or as a volunteer experience
-
- **Get experience:** Ask your boss or go for an internship for a small project that you can manage within six months
-
- **Gain education and training**: Finish your degree within two years

6. Follow Your Career Plan.

Now that you have created your career plan and designed the required steps to achieve them. It's time to follow the written plan. Don't just write down your plan and be happy that things will happen in their time. Tell your close ones and people about it and get their feedback, guidance, and support.

7. Review and Update Your Career Plan.

There can be a possibility that you are stuck and want to change your plan or mind. Do not get distressed or disheartened.

Review it again your career plan and makes changes as needed. Take a different path if the set path is not working. Modify your activities to reach your goals.

Always remember the world of work is changing very fast and so can you.

Rethink and remember that a Career is a lifelong journey.

CHAPTER FIVE

CAREER CLUSTER

There is a plethora of career options available in today's dynamic market.

But where do you start?

With more than 800+ career descriptions the choice for the best suited goes for a toss.

Here is where career cluster comes as a savior

Career clusters help to organize your search. Career clusters help you to find your way to more than 60 industries and 500 careers. A career cluster is a group of occupations with similar features.

There is 16 career cluster that can help you choose the most suitable path which can guide you for your successful career journey.

The 16 clusters are the exploration stage for early-stage career decisions and are divided based on the nature of the work.

There are mainly six career paths. It is further divided into career pathways.

SIX CAREER PATH

NATURE PATH	**BUSINESS PATH**
BUILDING PATH	**CREATIVE PATH**
HELPING PATH	**HEALTH PATH**

A. Nature Path

This path is related to the development of natural resources and agriculture. It requires the capability to work in an isolated location, in the outdoors, and in demanding weather conditions. People in this career work in forests, farms, nurseries, oceans, mines, forests, etc. The Cluster in this Path are highlighted below.

1. Agriculture, Natural, and Food Resources

It involves work to produce food, plants, animals, and crops. The Career Pathways in this cluster are as follows

Agribusiness: This pathway comprises work of coordination of all activities like the production, processing, marketing, distribution, financing and development, plant, and animal products.

Animal Systems: This pathway includes work related to the raising and caring of animals and developing more efficient ways of producing and processing meat, poultry, eggs, and dairy products.

Food products and processing: This pathway includes occupations involved in food production, finding food sources, and developing ways to process, preserve, package or store food according to consumer needs.

Environmental Service: This pathway includes work like waste management, research, quality control, recycling, waste, and air pollution control

Natural Resources: This pathway includes occupations that develop, use, maintain, and manage natural resources. Work might relate to recreation, wildlife, conservation, mining, or oil drilling.

Plant pathway: This pathway includes work related to growing food, and fiber crops, and the study of plants and their growth for conserving natural resources and maintaining the environment. This includes genetic engineering. The subject and streams in demand for this cluster are highlighted below.

SUBJECTS & STREAMS

Science	Mathematics
Agriculture	Biology
Humanities	Chemistry
Biotechnology	Geography
Physics	Earth Sciences

The specific courses suited for this cluster

GLOBAL COURSES	INDIAN COURSES
Natural Sciences	Engineering
Arts	Humanities
Engineering and Technology	Social Science
Humanities	Science

B. Building Path

This includes architecture and construction industry, electronics, manufacturing technology, production and repairs, engineering technology and related fields, transportation, etc.

This path is perfect for people who're good with their hands and enjoy working with mechanics. The clusters in this include the following

2. Manufacturing

It means designing a new product, deciding on how the product can be made, and ultimately making and producing the same. The pathways that come under this category are enumerated below

Maintenance and installation: This pathway include work for preventive maintenance procedures for machines, tools, and equipment.

Manufacturing production process: This pathway includes work responsible for product design and design of the manufacturing process.

Production: This pathway includes work-related for the making or assembling of electronic parts, constructing, or assembling modular housing, performing welding jobs, or printing various materials.

Quality assurance pathway includes work to assure that standards and procedures are adhered, and performance requirements are met by monitoring and maintaining the quality of parts and manufacturing processes.

The subject and streams in demand for this cluster are highlighted below.

SUBJECTS & STREAMS

Science	Mathematics
Physics	Humanities
Chemistry	Commerce
Physics	Languages / Literature (Arts)

The specific courses suited for this cluster

GLOBAL COURSES	INDIAN COURSES
Art and Design	Engineering
Engineering & Technology.	Humanities

Industries Pertinent for this Cluster.

GLOBAL INDUSTRY	INDIAN INDUSTRY/SECTOR
Manufacturing	Chemical
Information	Textile and Handlooms
Insurance	Iron & Steel
Finance	Textile
	Leather
	Automotive

3. Transportation, distribution, and logistics

These are related to moving people and products by road, air, rail, and water. The pathways in this cluster are given below

Facility and maintenance: This pathway include work related to the maintenance, repair, and servicing of vehicles and transportation facilities.

Health, safety, and environmental management: This pathway includes work for assessing and managing risks associated with safety and environmental issues.

Logistics planning and management: This pathway includes work for planning, management, and control of the physical distribution of materials, products, and people.

Transportation systems/infrastructure planning, management, and regulation: This pathway includes work related to all aspects of the design and operation of public transportation system, road, air, sea, and rail.

Warehousing and distribution: This pathway include work at the ports, terminals, warehouses, and other types of facilities for the operation of transportation and distribution facilities

The subject and streams in demand for this cluster are highlighted below.

SUBJECTS & STREAMS

Science	Mathematics
Physics	Transportation
Chemistry	Commerce
Economics	Supply Chain
Warehousing	

The specific courses suited for this cluster

GLOBAL COURSES	INDIAN COURSES
Business Studies	BBA/MBA
Management Studies	Hotel Management.
Engineering	Engineering
Technology	Commerce
Hospitality	

Industries Pertinent for this Cluster.

GLOBAL INDUSTRY	INDIAN INDUSTRY/SECTOR
Transportation& Warehousing	Warehousing
Utilities	Retail
Management	Aviation
	Shipping
	Automotive

4. Science, Technology, Engineering, and Mathematics

Careers in the STEM-Science, technology, engineering, and mathematics cluster involve working on scientific research and planning and designing products and systems.

Engineering and technology: This pathway involve works to use mathematics, science, and technology concepts to find problems quantitatively in projects like the design and, development of various technologies.

The subject and streams in demand for this cluster are highlighted below.

SUBJECTS & STREAMS

Science	Mathematics
Physics	Chemistry
Biology	Bioengineering
Graphics	Electronics
Computer Networking	

The specific courses suited for this cluster

GLOBAL COURSES	INDIAN COURSES
Education	BCA/MCA
Engineering	Education & Training
Natural Sciences	Engineering

Industries Pertinent for this Cluster.

GLOBAL INDUSTRY	INDIAN INDUSTRY/SECTOR
Manufacturing	Aviation & Automotive
Automotive	Iron and Steel
Environmental Science	Environmental Science

5. Architecture and construction

This cluster means a different kind of work on buildings and infrastructures like buildings, highways, bridges, and houses.

Construction includes work to build homes, or building, recreational, industrial, and office facilities. Includes flyers, highways, streets, bridges, tunnels, and airports.

Design and pre-construction: This pathway is the work related to the management and planning of the building and construction project process.

Maintenance and operations: This pathway include occupations that unload, inspect, install, and repair equipment and machinery.

The subject and streams in demand for this cluster are highlighted below.

GLOBAL INDUSTRY	INDIAN INDUSTRY/SECTOR
Construction	Construction
Real Estate	Real Estate
Utilities	Utilities
Infrastructure	Infrastructure

The specific courses suited for this cluster.

GLOBAL COURSES	INDIAN COURSES
Business & Management Studies	BBA/MBA
Art & Design	Commerce
Accounting	Engineering
Finance	Architecture

Industries Pertinent for this cluster.

GLOBAL INDUSTRY	INDIAN INDUSTRY/SECTOR
Construction	Construction
Real Estate	Real Estate
Utilities	Utilities
Infrastructure	Infrastructure

C. Business Path

Business Path includes the work or occupation of running and efficiently managing the enterprises involved in commercial activities. Marketing, Sales, Finance, and Information Technology can be included in this path. This is suitable for people who are good and at networking, leadership.

There is a gamut of careers that are available in business as well as Information Technology. There are four clusters in this career path.

6. Information technology

This cluster involves the work with computer hardware, software, multimedia, or network systems.

Information support and services include works related to information technology including implementing computer systems and software, database management, providing technical assistance, and managing information systems.

Network systems: This pathway includes works related to network analysis, planning, and implementation, including design, installation, maintenance, and management of network systems.

Programming and software development: This pathway includes works that involve the design, development, implementation, and maintenance of computer systems and software, requiring knowledge of computer operating systems, programming languages, and software development.

The Interactive Media, web, and digital communication: This pathway includes work in the creation, designing, and production of interactive multimedia products and services, including the development of digitally generated or computer-enhanced media used in business, training, entertainment, communications, and marketing.

The subject and streams in demand for this cluster are highlighted below.

SUBJECTS & STREAMS

Science	Commerce
Mathematics	Humanities
Computer Science	Communications
Graphics Design	Web Technology
Multimedia	Refrigeration

The specific courses suited for this cluster

GLOBAL COURSES	INDIAN COURSES
Art & Design	Engineering
Engineering	BCA/MCA
Technology	BBA/MBA
Business & Management Studies	

Industries Pertinent for this Cluster.

GLOBAL INDUSTRY	INDIAN INDUSTRY/SECTOR
Information Technology	IT-ITES
Infrastructure	Life Sciences
	Infrastructure

7. Business, Management, and Administration

This cluster involve work to provide the required leadership and support to make a business run. The Pathways, subject, streams, courses, and linked industry are highlighted below.

Business information management: This pathway includes the work needed to provide a bridge between business processes and information technology processes.

Business finance: This pathway includes works to run and implement policy and strategy for an organization's capital, budgeting, acquisition and investment, financial analysis, planning, funding, accounting, and taxation.

General management: This pathway includes occupations that plan, organize, coordinate, direct, control, and evaluate all or part of a business needed to produce or provide a business' goods and/or services.

Human resources management: This pathway comprises work on staffing activities, recruitment, selection, orientation, training, development, appraisal, compensation, and welfare of the organization's employees.

Marketing: This pathway covers work related to management, operations, and marketing activities that include marketing research, sales, advertising, promotions, or public relations in businesses, nonprofit institutions, and other organizations.

The subject and streams in demand for this cluster are highlighted below.

SUBJECTS & STREAMS

Science	Informatics Practices
Economics	Commerce
Computer Science	Entrepreneurship
Business Studies	Accounting
Mathematics	

The specific courses suited for this cluster.

GLOBAL COURSES	INDIAN COURSES
Accounting & Finance	BBA/MBA
Business & Management Studies	Commerce & Accounts
Arts & Humanities	Engineering
Engineering & Technology	Humanities & Social Science
Communication & Media Studies	Mass Communication
Hospitality & Leisure Management	Tourism Hotel Management

Industries Pertinent for this Cluster.

GLOBAL INDUSTRY	INDIAN INDUSTRY/SECTOR
Management of Companies and Enterprises	Apparel
Retail Trade	BFSI
Real Estate and Rental and Leasing	Automotive
Accommodation and Food Services	Media and Entertainment

8. Marketing and Sales

This clusters mainly include businesses to sell products and services. The Pathways, streams, subjects, courses, and linked industry, are highlighted below

Marketing communications pathway includes workers who plan, coordinate, and implement marketing strategies, advertising, promotion, and public relations activity

Market research is the pathway that includes occupations that collect and analyze different types of information to design new products, to predict sales, and to position strategies against its competitors.

Buying and merchandising pathway involve work associated with getting products into the hands of customers, including planning, buying, displaying, forecasting, selling, and providing better customer service.

Sales and marketing pathway comprises work in the act of convincing individual consumers or businesses to purchase goods and services.

E-Marketing is the pathway that includes occupations for online selling, search engine optimization, and social media marketing.

The subject and streams in demand for this cluster are highlighted below.

SUBJECTS & STREAMS

Science	Sociology
Commerce	Economics
Humanities	Mathematics
Biology	Languages / Literature
Psychology	Sales and Marketing
Merchandising	Media Communications
Computer Science	Informatics Practices

The specific courses suited for this cluster

GLOBAL COURSES	INDIAN COURSES
Accounting & Finance	BBA/MBA
Business & Management Studies	Commerce & Accounts
Arts & Humanities	Engineering
Engineering & Technology	Humanities & Social Science

Industries Pertinent for this Cluster.

GLOBAL INDUSTRY	INDIAN INDUSTRY/SECTOR
Management of Companies and Enterprises	Real Estate
Retail Trade	BFSI
Real Estate and Rental and Leasing	Automotive
Wholesale Trade	Media and Entertainment
Administrative and Support Services	Mining

9. Finance

This cluster covers work to keep track of money for financial planning, banking, or insurance. The Pathways, streams, subjects, courses, and linked industry, are highlighted below

Banking and related services pathway includes occupations concerned with credit cards, cash management, short-term investments, mortgages and other loans, and bill payment. This also includes accepting deposits, lending funds, and extending credit either through traditional banking institutions or via insurance companies, brokerage houses, or the Internet.

Business and financial planning pathway includes work on policymaking and strategy building for an organization's capital, budgeting, acquisition and investment, financial planning, funding, dividends, and taxation.

Insurance services pathway comprises work to deliver services to transfer risk from an individual or business to an insurance company to protect financial losses of the individuals and businesses.

Financial and investment planning pathway covers the work to support the flow of funds from investors to companies and institutions.

The subject and streams in demand for this cluster are highlighted below.

SUBJECTS & STREAMS

Science	Banking /
Financial Services	Business Law
Accounting	Mathematics
Economic	Commerce

The specific courses suited for this cluster

GLOBAL COURSES	INDIAN COURSES
Accounting & Finance	BBA/MBA
Business & Management Studies	Commerce & Accounts
Natural Sciences	Engineering
Engineering & Technology	Science

Industries Pertinent for this Cluster.

GLOBAL INDUSTRY	INDIAN INDUSTRY/SECTOR
Management of Companies and Enterprises	Real Estate
Finance and Insurance	BFSI
Real Estate and Rental and Leasing	Self-Employed
Self-Employed	

D. Creative Path

The creative path is primarily the Arts and communications. This career has one thing in common and that is creativity.

This path includes careers that encompass creative and imaginative thinkers to express themselves through various forms of designs, language and literature, and all forms of media. This consists of domains such as TV, radio, journalism, advertising, film, and digital media, public relations. The clusters in this Path

10. Arts, audio & video technology, and communications

This cluster comprises of creativity and talent. This consists of work as a performer or artist.

Audio and video technology and film pathway encompasses works to sell, design, install, integrate, operate, and repair the equipment of audio-visual communications. This includes dispensing sound, video, and data in venues like offices, convention centers, classrooms, theme parks, and stadiums.

Journalism and broadcasting pathway includes workers who like to research and write and produce news stories or broadcasts. This also includes publishing and writing.

Performing arts pathway consists of work that helps in the creation, production, and development of theatrical and musical performances.

Printing technology pathway includes occupations involved in press and binding. Work transforms text and pictures or uses digital technology for graphics, layout, or printing.

Telecommunications pathway comprises of work needed for interaction between computers and communications equipment. The workers install or repair data, graphics, video, and digital equipment.

Visual arts pathway consists of work in art creation like painting, sculpting, illustrating, fashion, or floral design, the use of an assortment of materials, including oils, pen, pencils, watercolors, acrylics, pastels, ink, photography, plaster, and clay, textiles, plants.

The subject and streams in demand for this cluster are highlighted below.

SUBJECTS & STREAMS

Humanities	Speech & Drama
Science	Home Science
Commerce	Fine Arts
Graphic Design	Languages / Literature
Printing Technology	Music
Fashion Studies	Creative Writing
Translation Studies	Mass Media Studies
Multimedia	

The specific courses suited for this cluster

GLOBAL COURSES	INDIAN COURSES
Performing Arts	BBA/MBA
Hospitality & Leisure Management	Tourism Hotel Management
Communication & Media Studies	Fine Arts
Education & Training	Mass Communication
Engineering & Technology	Education

Industries Pertinent for this Cluster.

GLOBAL INDUSTRY	INDIAN INDUSTRY/SECTOR
Information	Media and Entertainment
Arts Entertainment and Recreation	Telecom

E. Helping Path

Helping path include Human services which encompass occupations, covering elements of education, psychology, justice studies, hospitality, and other services, etc. Working in this pathway needs a great sense of compassion and patience. The clusters in this path are mainly five.

11. Human Services

You can explore Pathways and linked industries, careers, and courses below.

Counseling and mental health services pathway comprises work to assist people with personal, family, educational, mental health, and career decisions and problems. The work can be in hospitals, clinics, and schools.

Early childhood development and services pathway includes occupations related to the nurturing or teaching of infants and young children in childcare centers, nursery schools, preschools, public schools, private households, and before- and after-school programs.

Family and community services pathway consists of occupations to help the disabled, elderly, or other underrepresented populations to secure housing, education, employment, financial assistance, or other social services

Personal care services pathway covers occupations that provide services to an individual's physical care, including spa, cosmetic, fitness, and funeral services.

The subject and streams in demand for this cluster are highlighted below.

SUBJECTS & STREAMS

Humanities	Commerce
Languages / Literature	Sociology
Psychology	Philosophy
Home Science	Foreign Languages
Social Work	Physical Education

The specific courses suited for this cluster

GLOBAL COURSES	INDIAN COURSES
Arts & Humanities	Humanities & Social Science
Hospitality & Leisure Management	Tourism Hotel Management
Performing Arts	BBA/MBA
Business & Management Studies	Fine Arts

Industries Pertinent for this Cluster.

GLOBAL INDUSTRY	INDIAN INDUSTRY/SECTOR
Health Care and Social Assistance	Apparel
Self-Employed	Beauty and Wellness
Retail Trade	Gem and Jewelry
Other Services-Except Public Administration	Leather
Government	Organized Retail

12. Hospitality and tourism

This cluster involves work to help people enjoy vacations and entertainment. You can explore Pathways and linked industries, careers, and courses below.

Lodging pathway includes work related to the operation of lodging facilities. This also includes the care of guests who use these facilities.

Recreation and amusements pathway includes work like the operation and maintenance of facilities, and services for recreation or amusement. It Includes amusement parks, outdoor areas, arcades, performance areas, museums etc.

Restaurants and food and beverage services pathway includes work to perform a variety of tasks to promote guest services in eating and drinking establishments.

Travel and tourism pathway includes occupations focused on the packaging, promotion, and delivery of a traveler's experiences. This Include operating a facility, developing promotional materials, planning trips and events, and managing a customer's travel plans.

The subject and streams in demand for this cluster are highlighted below.

SUBJECTS & STREAMS

Humanities	Science
Foreign Languages	Political Science
History	Languages / Literature
Social Studies	Beauty / Cosmetics
Marketing	Food & Beverages

The specific courses suited for this cluster

GLOBAL COURSES	INDIAN COURSES
Arts & Humanities	Humanities & Social Science
Hospitality & Leisure Management	Tourism Hotel Management
Performing Arts	BBA/MBA
Business & Management Studies	Fine Arts

Industries Pertinent for this Cluster.

GLOBAL INDUSTRY	INDIAN INDUSTRY/SECTOR
Self-Employed	Beauty & Wellness
Accommodation and Food Services	Tourism and Hospitality
Arts Entertainment and Recreation	Food Industry
Transportation and Warehousing	Sports, Physical Education, Fitness and Leisure

13. Education and training

This cluster helps in guiding and training people. You can explore Pathways and linked industries, careers, and courses below.

Administration and administrative support pathway work to provide direction, day-to-day management, and support of educational activities in schools, preschools, childcare centers, colleges, universities, businesses and industries, and job training and community service organizations.

Professional support services pathway covers work that assists people in education and training with personal and family needs, career decision making, mental health assistance, and educational goals.

Teaching and training pathway includes the work that assists in the delivery of instructional materials or lessons in classrooms, workshops, or via online and distance technology. This includes individual and group children, adults, and professionals.

The subject and streams in demand for this cluster are highlighted below.

SUBJECTS & STREAMS

Humanities	Psychology
Science	Sociology
Commerce	Philosophy
Languages / Literature	Mathematics
Social Studies	Political Science
Physical Education	History
Multimedia	Web Technology

The specific courses suited for this cluster

GLOBAL COURSES	INDIAN COURSES
Education & Training	Education
Arts & Humanities	Humanities & Social Science
Business & Management Studies	BBA/MBA

Industries Pertinent for this Cluster.

GLOBAL INDUSTRY	INDIAN INDUSTRY/SECTOR
Educational Services	Education Training and Research
Government	Sports, Physical Education
	Fitness and Leisure

14. Government and Public administration

This cluster consists of work to enforce the law either at the local, state, or national level. You can explore Pathways and linked industries, careers, and courses below

Governance pathway includes work in making and executing public policy by working with officials, and constituents. It Includes elected officials or appointed to government positions and support staff.

Public management and administration pathway involve the work to regulate the policies that manage the stewardship of public resources largely used by government agencies, public corporations, etc. This includes budgeting, personnel management, and procurement.

Revenue and taxation pathway comprises of work so that governments obtain revenues from businesses and citizens by collecting tax, reviewing tax returns, conducting audits, monitoring taxes payable, and collecting overdue tax.

National security pathway includes work focused on keeping the country's people, institutions, technology, and economy safe from physical or cyber-attack.

The subject and streams in demand for this cluster are highlighted below.

SUBJECTS & STREAMS

Humanities	Science
Mathematics	Political Science
History	Languages / Literature
Sociology	Psychology
Philosophy	History
Economics	Foreign Languages

The specific courses suited for this cluster

GLOBAL COURSES	INDIAN COURSES
Arts & Humanities	Humanities & Social Science
Law	Law
Engineering & Technology	BBA/MBA
Business & Management Studies	Engineering

Industries Pertinent for this Cluster.

GLOBAL INDUSTRY	INDIAN INDUSTRY/SECTOR
Government	Healthcare
Utilities	Legislators
Administrative and Support Services	Office Administration and Facility Management
Mining Quarrying and Oil and Gas Extraction	Postal Services
	Power

15. *Law, public safety, corrections, and security*

This cluster works to guard the public and enforce the law as police officers or security guards. You can explore Pathways and linked industries, careers, and courses below.

Correction services pathway includes the job of overseeing individuals who have been arrested and are awaiting trial, or who have been convicted of a crime and sentenced to serve time in a jail, reformatory, or penitentiary.

Law enforcement services pathway includes work to protect the lives and property of community members, by controlling traffic, investigating crimes, enforcing laws and ordinances, arresting, and processing suspected criminals.

Legal services pathway includes work of monitoring, implementing, and upholding of the laws and regulations.

Security and protective services pathway consist of work for the protection of people or property in public buildings. The work can be in factories, laboratories, museums, shopping malls, government buildings, etc.

The subject and streams in demand for this cluster are highlighted below.

SUBJECTS & STREAMS

Humanities	Psychology
Science	Philosophy
Sociology	Political Science
Mathematics	History
Languages / Literature	Law Enforcement
Physical Education	Law

The specific courses suited for this cluster

GLOBAL COURSES	INDIAN COURSES
Law	Law
Natural Sciences	Science

Industries Pertinent for this Cluster.

GLOBAL INDUSTRY	INDIAN INDUSTRY/SECTOR
Professional Scientific	Judiciary
Technical Services	Legislators
Government	Legal Activities
	Private Security

F. Health Path

Health services are given by medical professionals and organizations, and health care workers to patients, families, and communities. These include services like prevention and treatment of physical and mental illnesses, diseases, and injuries, nutritional guidance, rehabilitation therapy, and home care. The cluster in this path is health science.

16. Health Science

Health science cluster comprises work to promote health, wellness, and treating illness. You can explore pathways and linked industries, careers, and courses below.

Biotechnology research and development pathway comprises work in bioscience research and development. Workers study diseases to discover new treatments or invent medical devices used to directly assist patients

Diagnostic services pathway includes covers tests and evaluations that help in the detection, diagnosis, and treatment of diseases or injuries.

Support services pathway includes job to interact with patients or the public to provide a therapeutic environment. This includes technical and professional careers.

Health informatics pathway consists of work for managing health care agencies, patient data and information, financial information, and computer applications related to health care processes and procedures.

Therapeutic services pathway focuses mainly on the health status of patients over the time through health education information, direct care, treatment, and counseling.

The subject and streams in demand for this cluster are highlighted below.

SUBJECTS & STREAMS

Humanities	Biology
Science	Biotechnology
Chemistry	Physics
Mathematics	Home Science
Languages / Literature	Physical Education

The specific courses suited for this cluster.

GLOBAL COURSES	INDIAN COURSES
Arts & Humanities	Medicine
Natural Sciences	Humanities & Social Science
Science	BCA/MCA

Industries Pertinent for this Cluster.

GLOBAL INDUSTRY	INDIAN INDUSTRY/SECTOR
Health Care and Social Assistance	Healthcare
Legal Activities	Life Sciences
	Private Security

CHAPTER SIX

CAREER RESEARCH

What is Career research?

Career research is the act of exploring potential career opportunities to determine which field is the best suitable for you.

What is the purpose of career research?

Career Research helps individuals identify the skills they will need to succeed.

Career research exposes young people and professionals to the world of work and to many exciting jobs that are available.

Benefits of Career Research

It helps to make more informed decisions from others' expertise and experience. In the case of making career decisions Career Research is one way that renders support and constructive guidance in several ways:

Discovers your strength and weakness.

1. Sets objectives and goals.
2. Decides the right career
3. Provides good resources.
4. Curtails the frustration and confusion.
5. Gives useful support and motivation

.

How to conduct Career Research.

How to conduct Career Research is one important activity regardless of where you are in your career. There are various ways where you can gather information and execute it. You can use online resources to fetch information about industries. You can connect with professionals and get the details and realities of the path that interests you.

Career Research Process is an ongoing process that occurs in several steps. This is not a one-time job. This consists of the following stages:

Stage 1

Brainstorming

It may sound like a simple suggestion, but it is a good first move. Make two lists of things, one you like to do and two you do not like to do.

For example, do they like Geography class but hate math class or vice versa?

- Do you like to work in groups, or do you prefer to work alone?
- Do you like to work indoors or outdoors?

Stage 2

Assessment tests

Assessment tests will help you to self-assess yourself on various traits like your interests, skill sets, personality, etc. You can perform this test with the help of several tools and techniques. Some examples are:

- *Intelligence Quotient (IQ) Test*
- *Emotional Quotient (EQ) Test*
- *Adversity Quotient (AQ) Test*
- *Aptitude Test & Personality Test includes the following tests*

- *Myers-Briggs Type Indicator (MBTI) /16 Personalities Test.*
- *Test Color*
- *DiSC Assessments*
- *Berkeley Emotional Intelligence Test*
- *PATH Assessment*

The result of this test gives you a detailed description of each intelligence. Apart from all other test assessments, the most important test is the Psychometric Test.

A psychometric test is an assessment to evaluate an individual's overall performance and is not restricted to skills, abilities, personality traits, and Job potential.

The best Psychometric test used widely are listed below:

- *The Meyer-Briggs Type Indicator (MBTI)*
- *16 Personalities Factor*
- *DiSC*
- *Logical Reasoning Assessment*
- *Numerical Reasoning Assessment*
- *Verbal Reasoning Assessment*

Once you have successfully completed these assessment tests. You come up with 7-10 Career options. This collected information will help you in drawing a decision.

It is highly recommended that at this stage you take guidance from your Parents, Teachers, Siblings, Mentor, etc.

Now, you need to narrow down your choices to 1-to 2 Career options. Just, for instance, you came up with a final career option of pursuing a career as a doctor or Lawyer. The next steps are of paramount importance.

Stage 3

Get into the Shoes of a Potential Career

You must get into the shoes of a potential career to get an insight into that Career. This is called *Job shadowing.*

This is the practice of working with a professional in the career of your choice.

You spend several hours with the professional to *"shadow"* them and see exactly what they do daily.

You can explore your own ways to get them and then set up individual job shadowing experiences.

You can job shadow yourself by approaching these professionals (e.g., Doctor or Lawyer) and spend 1-2 days with them.

Take a taste of their work, their daily activities, their responsibilities, and their sense of satisfaction.

Make a list of questions and ask them what made them select this Career or Profession and what kind of preparation they have taken to get into this field. Get the below-mentioned facts and figures.

- *Job description*
- *Employers or types of employers*
- *Salary ranges*
- *Expected job growth over the next few years*
- *Educational requirements*
- *Job's locations*

Also get to know about their skillset, interest, abilities, natural inclination, and hobbies. Get in deeper with further questions

1. How did the person train for the job?
2. What does the person like best about their job?
3. What do people dislike about their job?
4. What has the person learned that they wish they had known before pursuing the career?
5. What advice does the professional have concerning on what one should and should not do in pursuit of the career?

The above activity will be a real experience for you and much of your confusion will be resolved here. Now that you have collected the responses regarding the career from the horse's mouth.

Make a report of it, study it, get in-depth, and analyze it.

Stage 4

Mapping and Overlapping

Now you need to map the information. Map the collected information from these professionals (e.g., Doctors and Lawyers) with the collected information from your self-assessment.

Once done with mapping, find the overlapping section of the information.

Overlapping the data will help you in getting the best possible result.

This will draw a conclusion for you.

Now, for example, you came to the conclusion that you want to pursue Law as your career. Becoming a Lawyer is your Goal. Your goals are finalized.

It's time for you to take action to reach that goal.

Stage 5

Taking Action

Take action by making a roadmap to reach the set goal. For e.g. You finalized to become a Lawyer.

Find the stream, majors, and core subjects for pursuing law as a career.

What are the examinations needed to take for getting into Law School or Colleges? Check out the eligibility criterion.

List out the names best Colleges and Universities. Find out the application and selection process. Understand their scholarship and financial aid.

Other ways to find career information include:

a. Watch career videos
b. Read interviews about specific careers
c. Attend career-specific networking events or career fairs.
d. Visit a worksite.
e. Intern in a position
f. Look through detailed career profiles

g. Find high-demand jobs

Before Conclusion: As you learn more and move ahead with a particular career path, make sure to stop and reflect on what you have learned.
Ask yourself these questions:

a. Am I still interested in this career path?
b. What excites me the most about this role/industry?
c. What concerns do I have about this line of work?
d. Can I work in this environment?
e. Will this path capitalize on my strengths?
f. Does this path align with my values?
g. What skills do I need to develop?
h. What information am I still missing?
a. Do I need to connect to Career Counselor or Industry Advisors?

Stage 6

Conclusion

Career Research is the most ignored practice by Students, Parents, Guardians, and Professionals. Though people do not practice it, it should be considered one of the vital practice.

Hope these have given you an in-depth knowledge of how to conduct your Career Research

It is advisable for each of you to go through the process and get an insight before jumping into the final decision

BONUS CHAPTER: HOTTEST CAREER ACROSS THE GLOBE

There are various courses available in the market for a bright and successful career. Selecting the best course out of the rest is a tough task.

Courses leading to its subsequent career are very important. It is the individual's choice and inclination that plays a vital role to fix it.

Here are the top 5 hottest jobs across the globe for a successful and lucrative career path. Find out the details highlighted below:

1. ARTIFICIAL INTELLIGENCE

Artificial intelligence (AI) is the ability of a computer, or a robot controlled by a computer to do tasks that are usually done by humans because they require human intelligence and discernment.

Life with technology is almost impossible. Technology is ruling the world.

It is estimated that the AI market will be a major player in this field. AI is growing at a rate of 43%. This is the reason why the demand and scope of AI professionals have increased manifold.

Day to day examples of Artificial Intelligence

Artificial Intelligence is commonly used in day-to-day activities, but you may not be aware of this. Below mentioned are example of daily work where the concept of artificial intelligence is used.

- E-Payments
- Digital Assistants
- Chatbots
- Google Maps
- Face Detection
- Face Recognition

Who is eligible for taking up Artificial Intelligence courses and jobs?

- Candidates with a sound knowledge of coding languages such as Python, Natural Language Processing, and Machine learning algorithms will be preferred.
- Candidates who have completed -BTech Artificial Intelligence, BTech in Computer Science- Artificial Intelligence & Machine Learning, and MTech in Artificial Intelligence are fully eligible to continue with the course of Artificial Intelligence.
- Candidates with problem-solving acumen can go for this course.
- Candidates with a good hold in mathematics must definitely go for this course.

Job Role after completing this course

There are various jobs available in different companies across the globe after completing this course. Some of the most sought are mentioned below:

- Data Analyst
- Big Data Analyst
- Data Engineer
- Machine Learning Engineer

Top Recruiters looking for Artificial Intelligence Profile

Listed below are the name of the few recruiters who take individuals with artificial intelligence knowledge and degrees. There are various other companies that are interested in hiring professionals with this background and courses.

- Google
- American Express
- Amazon
- Myntra
- Flipkart
- Adobe
- Genpact
- Mobikwik

2. MACHINE LEARNING

Machine learning is an application of artificial intelligence (AI) that provides systems the ability to automatically learn and improve from experience without being clearly programmed. Machine learning focuses on computer program development that can access data and use it to learn on their own.

Machine learning is a modern-day innovation that helps in many professionals and industrial processes as well as in daily activities.

MI helps in using the statistical tools and techniques to make intelligent computer systems learn from the database available. Machine learning is artificial intelligence, but Artificial intelligence is not Machine learning. Machine learning is a subset of Artificial Learning (AI).

Day to day examples of Machine Learning

Machine Learning is commonly used in day-to-day activities, but you may not be aware of this. Below mentioned are examples of daily work where the concept of Machine Learning is used.

- Medical diagnosis.
- Image and face recognition
- Speech recognition
- Self-driving cars
- Virtual assistant- Siri, Alexa.

Who is eligible for taking up Machine Learning courses and jobs?

Machine learning is a hot course with lots of scopes and opportunities. Therefore, this course can be taken seriously for making a career.

There is no fixed qualification to pursue this course. But one must possess knowledge of basic computer technology and a good understanding with a degree in mathematics can take up this course.

- Candidates should have a basic knowledge of Multivariate Calculus, Linear Algebra, Python, and Statistics.
- Candidates should have a basic knowledge of Machine Learning, such as the terminologies of machine learning and machine learning types.
- Candidates should have a strong command of working on data collection, data cleaning, data integration, and data pre-processing.

Job Role after completing this course

There are various jobs available in different companies across the globe after completing this course. Some of the most sought are mentioned below:

- Machine Learning Engine
- Software Engineer
- Data Scientist
- Data Analyst
- Data Architect
- Software Developer
- Research Scientist
- Data Science Manager

Top Recruiters looking for Machine Learning Profile

Listed below are the name of the few recruiters who take individuals with machine learning knowledge and degrees. There are various other companies that are interested in hiring professionals with this background and courses.

- Google
- Amazon
- Adobe
- Uber
- Facebook
- Apple
- Microsoft

3. BIG DATA

Big Data is an extremely large set of data- both structured and unstructured that a business is overloaded with on a day-to-day basis.

Big data is data with a very large size and is very complex that traditional data management tools cannot store it or process it efficiently. Big data is a database with a huge size. Big Data is used to analyze and systematically extract information from too large and complex data.

Day to day examples of Big Data

Big Data is commonly used in day-to-day activities, but you may not be aware of this. Below mentioned are examples of daily work where the concept of big data is used.

- Facebook user profile
- Google search index
- Stock Exchanges
- Online shopping

Who is eligible for taking up Big Data courses and jobs?

The world is full of organized, unorganized, structured, semi-structured, and unstructured data. The true meaning of these data can be only made through various analyses etc. Therefore, the demand for professionals who can understand this big data is increasing exponentially. This is a booming sector with lots of scope and opportunities.

There is no hard and fast rule to be eligible to continue with the course of a big data professional. However, a fair understanding of mathematics, statistics, programming, and domain knowledge is needed to excel in this career. Also, a basic understanding of R/Python/Matlab/SAS programming will be very helpful.

Job Role after completing this course

There are various jobs available in different companies across the globe after completing this course. Some of the most sought are mentioned below:

- Big Data Analyst
- Big Data Architect
- Big Data Engineer
- Data Developer
- Data Scientist

Top Recruiters looking for Big Data Profile

Listed below are the name of the few recruiters who take individuals with big data knowledge and degrees. There are various other companies that are interested in hiring professionals with this background and courses.

- Amazon
- Flipkart
- IBM
- Walmart
- LinkedIn
- Deloitte

4. DATA SCIENCE

Data science is a multi- interdisciplinary subject or field which encompasses the processes and systems to extract knowledge or insights from data. The data can be in various forms, either structured or unstructured, to be evaluated with the use of mathematics, statistics, and computer science.

The main objective of data science is to take the information from the data to evaluate and use in making strategy, decision making, product development, and many more.

Day to examples of Data Science

Data Science is commonly used in day-to-day activities, but you may not be aware of this. Below mentioned are examples of daily work where the concept of data science is used.

- Gaming
- Face recognition
- Speech recognition
- Online shopping
- Internet searches
- Ecommerce

Who is eligible for taking up Data Science courses and jobs?

This sector is booming and will continue to grow in the near future. This has huge market potential as per several surveys conducted across the globe. A newcomer or a professional from a different profile like Marketing, IT, or Engineering can make a career in this.

- Candidates should have a fair knowledge of Mathematics, Computer Science, and Statistics is needed.
- Candidates should have a fair knowledge of data visualization like the access, retrieval, and presentation of the data.

- Candidates should have a fair knowledge of data analysis and hypothesis testing will be an added value.
- Candidates should have a fair knowledge of the languages like Java, Python, etc.

Job Role after completing this course

There are various jobs available in different companies across the globe after completing this course. Some of the most sought are mentioned below:

- Big Data Engineer
- Machine Learning Engineer
- Data Engineer/Data Architect
- Data Scientist
- Data Analysts
- Business Analysts

Top Recruiters looking for Data Science Profile

Listed below are the name of the few recruiters who take individuals with data science knowledge and degrees. There are various other companies that are interested in hiring professionals with this background and courses.

- Amazon
- Citrix
- LinkedIn
- IBM
- Walmart Labs
- Myntra
- Sigmoid
- Flipkart
- Couture

5. BLOCKCHAIN

Blockchain is a system of recording information or database in a way that makes it difficult or impossible to change, hack, or cheat the system. It is a database full of information that is stored electronically in systems.

Blockchain may look very complicated and complex, but the core concept of blockchain is quite simple and easy to understand. Blockchain is a type of Distributed Ledger Technology (DLT) with a cryptographic signature called a Hash.

Day to day examples of Blockchain

Blockchain is commonly used in day-to-day activities, but you may not be aware of this. Below mentioned are examples of daily work where the concept of blockchain is used.

- Cryptocurrency
- Voting machine
- Storing public data
- E-Commerce business

Who is eligible for taking up Blockchain courses and jobs?

Blockchain technology is one of the fastest-growing industries worldwide with incredible scope. Blockchain is the best technology that many industries will be using and implementing in the future. There are no hard and fast set criteria for pursuing this course.

- Candidates should have a basic knowledge of information technology, data security, and computer science. An understanding of distributed systems, networking, cryptography, and data structures would be a plus.
- Candidates should have fundamental skills and knowledge in the technical field.
- Candidates should have a basic understanding of Blockchain Security.
- Candidates should have a basic knowledge of blockchain platforms.
- Candidates should have a basic knowledge of Distributed Ledger expertise.

Job Role after completing this course

There are various jobs available in different companies across the globe after completing this course. Some of the most sought are mentioned below:

- Software Engineer
- Product Manager
- Risk Analyst
- Business Analyst
- Tech Architect
- Crypto Manager
- Blockchain Project Manager.
- Blockchain Quality Engineer.
- Blockchain Developer

Top Recruiters looking for Blockchain Profile

Listed below are the name of the few recruiters who take individuals with blockchain knowledge and degrees. There are various other companies that are interested in hiring professionals with this background and courses.

- TCS
- HCL
- IBM
- Visa
- Microsoft
- Deloitte
- Amazon
- Ernst & Young.

****

Conclusion

There are many courses available, but the one which is most suitable for you is of utmost importance.

It is always advisable to do proper career research before selecting any course or job.

This is the shaping stone of your career, which will stay with you for a long period of time. So, take a wise decision before opting for the one.

Thank you for owning this book. I hope this self-guided book was helpful for you. You deserve the best version of yours.

You deserve to be the successful person as you can be. This is an opportunity for growth.

Embrace it.

Finally, if you enjoyed this, then I'd like to ask you for a favor, would you be kind enough to leave a review for this book on Amazon? It'd be greatly appreciated!

!!!! Thank You and Good Luck !!!!

www.ingramcontent.com/pod-product-compliance
Lightning Source LLC
Chambersburg PA
CBHW031322130726
47988CB00007B/2940